SCHOLASTIC

READ & RESPOND

Bringing the best books to life in the classroom

BERLIE DOHERTY

STREET CHILD

COLLINS MODERN CLASSICS

FOR AGES 7–11

Published in the UK by Scholastic Education, 2019

Scholastic Distribution Centre, Bosworth Avenue, Tournament Fields, Warwick, CV34 6UQ

Scholastic Ireland, 89E Lagan Road, Dublin Industrial Estate, Glasnevin, Dublin, D11 HP5F

SCHOLASTIC and associated logos are trademarks and/or registered trademarks of Scholastic Inc.

www.scholastic.co.uk

© 2019 Scholastic

3 4 5 6 7 8 9   2 3 4 5 6 7 8 9 0 1
Printed and bound by Ashford Colour Press

The book is made of materials from well-managed,
FSC®-certified forests and other controlled sources.

A CIP catalogue record for this book is available from the British Library.
ISBN 978-1407-18251-3

Extracts from *The National Curriculum in England, English Programme of Study* © Crown Copyright. Reproduced under the terms of the Open Government Licence (OGL). http://www.nationalarchives.gov.uk/doc/open-government-licence/version/3

Due to the nature of the web, we cannot guarantee the content or links of any site mentioned. We strongly recommend that teachers check websites before using them in the classroom.

Authors Jillian Powell
Editorial team Rachel Morgan, Vicki Yates, Caroline Hale, Suzanne Adams
Series designers Neil Salt and Alice Duggan
Designer Alice Duggan
Illustrator Tanja Stevanovic / The Bright Agency

Acknowledgements
The publishers gratefully acknowledge permission to reproduce the following copyright material:
HarperCollins for the use of the extract text from Street Child by Berlie Doherty (HarperCollins, 1995). Text copyright © Berlie Doherty, 1993.

Every effort has been made to trace copyright holders for the works reproduced in this book, and the publishers apologise for any inadvertent omissions.

CONTENTS ▽

How to use Read & Respond in your classroom...

Read & Respond provides teaching ideas related to a specific well-loved children's book. Each Read & Respond book is divided into the following sections:

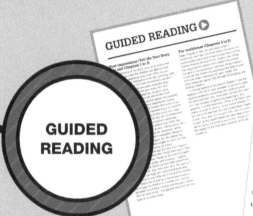

ABOUT THE BOOK AND AUTHOR

Gives you some background information about the book and the author.

GUIDED READING

Breaks the book down into sections and gives notes for using it with guided reading groups. A bookmark has been provided on page 12 containing comprehension questions. The children can be directed to refer to these as they read.

SHARED READING

Provides extracts from the children's book with associated notes for focused work. There is also one non-fiction extract that relates to the children's book.

GRAMMAR, PUNCTUATION & SPELLING

Provides word-level work related to the children's book so you can teach grammar, punctuation and spelling in context.

PLOT, CHARACTER & SETTING

Contains activity ideas focused on the plot, characters and the setting of the story.

TALK ABOUT IT

Has speaking and listening activities related to the children's book. These activities may be based directly on the children's book or be broadly based on the themes and concepts of the story.

GET WRITING

Provides writing activities related to the children's book. These activities may be based directly on the children's book or be broadly based on the themes and concepts of the story.

ASSESSMENT

Contains short activities that will help you assess whether the children have understood concepts and curriculum objectives. They are designed to be informal activities to feed into your planning.

> The titles are great fun to use and cover exactly the range of books that children most want to read. It makes it easy to explore texts fully and ensure the children want to keep on reading more.
>
> **Chris Flanagan, Year 5 Teacher, St Thomas of Canterbury Primary School**

Activities

The activities follow the same format:

- **Objective:** the objective for the lesson. It will be based upon a curriculum objective, but will often be more specific to the focus being covered.

- **What you need:** a list of resources you need to teach the lesson, including photocopiable pages.

- **What to do:** the activity notes.

- **Differentiation:** this is provided where specific and useful differentiation advice can be given to support and/or extend the learning in the activity. Differentiation by providing additional adult support has not been included as this will be at a teacher's discretion based upon specific children's needs and ability, as well as the availability of support.

The activities are numbered for reference within each section and should move through the text sequentially – so you can use the lesson while you are reading the book. Once you have read the book, most of the activities can be used in any order you wish.

CURRICULUM LINKS

Section	Activity	Curriculum objectives
Guided reading		Comprehension: To ask questions to improve their understanding.
Shared reading	1	Comprehension: To discuss and evaluate how authors use language, including figurative language.
	2	Comprehension: To explain and discuss their understanding of what they have read.
	3	Comprehension: To discuss and evaluate how authors use language, including figurative language.
	4	Spoken language: To ask relevant questions to extend their understanding and knowledge.
Grammar, punctuation & spelling	1	Vocabulary, grammar and punctuation: To use expanded noun phrases to convey complicated information concisely.
	2	Vocabulary, grammar and punctuation: To use passive verbs to affect the presentation of information in a sentence.
	3	Vocabulary, grammar and punctuation: To use the perfect form of verbs to mark relationships of time and cause.
	4	Vocabulary, grammar and punctuation: To use modal verbs... to indicate degrees of possibility.
	5	Transcription: To continue to distinguish between homophones and other words which are often confused.
	6	Transcription: To spell some words with 'silent' letters; to understand that the spelling of some words needs to be learned specifically.
Plot, character & setting	1	Comprehension: To identify and discuss themes and conventions in and across a wide range of writing; to make comparisons within and across books.
	2	Spoken language: To articulate and justify arguments and opinions.
	3	Comprehension: To explain and discuss their understanding of what they have read.
	4	Comprehension: To retrieve, record and present information from non-fiction.
	5	Comprehension: To summarise the main ideas drawn from more than one paragraph, identifying key details that support the main ideas.
	6	Comprehension: To draw inferences, such as inferring characters' feelings, thoughts and motives from their actions, and justifying inferences with evidence.
	7	Comprehension: To explain and discuss their understanding of what they have read.
	8	Comprehension: To predict what might happen from details stated and implied.

Section	Activity	Curriculum objectives
Talk about it	1	Comprehension: To ask questions to improve their understanding.
	2	Comprehension: To draw inferences... justifying inferences with evidence.
	3	Comprehension: To distinguish between statements of fact and opinion.
	4	Spoken language: To use spoken language to develop understanding through speculating, hypothesising, imagining and exploring ideas.
	5	Spoken language: To participate in discussions... and debates.
	6	Spoken language: To participate in... role play and improvisations.
Get writing	1	Spoken language: To prepare poems... to perform.
	2	Composition: To identify the audience for and purpose of the writing, selecting the appropriate form.
	3	Composition: To use... organisational and presentational devices to structure text and to guide the reader.
	4	Comprehension: To identify main ideas drawn from more than one paragraph and to summarise these.
	5	Comprehension: To predict what might happen from details stated and implied.
	6	Comprehension: To predict what might happen from details stated and implied.
Assessment	1	Comprehension: To identify and discuss themes and conventions in and across a wide range of writing.
	2	Composition: To identify the audience for and purpose of the writing, selecting the appropriate form and using other similar writing as models for their own.
	3	Comprehension: To identify main ideas drawn from more than one paragraph and to summarise these.
	4	Comprehension: To explain and discuss their understanding of what they have read.
	5	Comprehension: To ask questions to improve their understanding.
	6	Transcription: To understand that the spelling of some words needs to be learned specifically.

Key facts

Street Child

● **Author:**
Berlie Doherty

● **First published:**
1993

● **Awards:**
Nominated for the
Carnegie Medal and
shortlisted for the
Sheffield Award

● **Did you know?**
The author adapted *Street
Child* into a stage play
which was performed by
the Cotton Grass Theatre
Company with actors and
life-size puppets.

About the book

Jim Jarvis, the central character in Berlie Doherty's novel,
is based on the real boy who is believed to have inspired
'Doctor' Thomas Barnardo to set up his ragged schools
and, later, orphanages for homeless street children. The
philanthropist (who never actually completed his training to
qualify as a doctor yet was referred to as such) sent short
pamphlets containing notes on Jim and children like him
to prospective wealthy donors when he was trying to raise
money to fund his first orphanage. Doherty invented most
of the other characters and used extensive research into life
in Victorian London and social reform to create the setting
for her novel.

Street Child tells Jim's story, from the time when he
becomes homeless following the death of his mother, to
his rescue from the streets by Dr Barnardo (Barnie). Set in
the 1860s, the novel is packed with historical detail as we
follow Jim's adventures escaping from the bleak workhouse
and living life as a street child, skipping and dancing for the
crowds, until he is 'sold' to Grimy Nick, the cruel master
of a coal lighter which ferries coal along the River Thames.
Vulnerable and alone, Jim must invent his own inner voice to
become a 'bruvver' for himself, to keep his spirits alive as he
battles against those who maltreat and exploit him. When
he finally gets away from Nick and his dangerous dog Snipe,
Jim lives rough on the streets until he begins to attend the
classes at one of Barnardo's ragged schools and finds the
thing he most longs for – a safe home.

About the author

Berlie Doherty was born in Knotty Ash, Liverpool and
educated at Upton Hall Convent School before studying
English and Social Science at Durham University. While she
was training to be an English teacher, she wrote a short
story for Sheffield Radio and was then commissioned to
write for Schools Radio. She was a social worker and teacher
and wrote for the children's page of the *Liverpool Echo*,
before becoming a full-time writer in 1983. She says she
gets inspiration from things she reads or sees in her everyday
life, such as a painting in an art gallery which inspired her
novel *Granny was a Buffer Girl* (1987). She has written over
60 books for children, teenagers and adults, as well as plays
for radio, television and the theatre and libretti for children's
operas. Her novels have been translated into 20 languages
and have won many awards, including the Carnegie Medal
for *Granny was a Buffer Girl* (1986) and *Dear Nobody* (1991)
and the Writers' Guild Awards. She lives in Derbyshire and,
as well as writing, she enjoys visiting schools and libraries to
give talks and run workshops with young writers.

GUIDED READING ▶

First impressions (Tell Me Your Story, Jim and Chapters 1 to 3)

Start by looking at the book cover and reading the blurb. Discuss what the children can deduce from them. (It's an adventure story.) Ask: *What do you expect a story in that genre to be like?* (exciting, with ups and downs for the main character(s); possible dangers they have to overcome along the way)

Begin reading 'Tell me your story, Jim' and Chapter 1. Ask: *How does the narrative voice change?* (It changes from the first to the third person.) Explain that the author based the character of Jim on a real-life boy who inspired the famous Victorian philanthropist, Dr Thomas Barnardo, to set up his first orphanage for homeless boys. Jim told his story to Dr Barnardo (Barnie in the story) who used it in one of the pamphlets he sent out to prospective wealthy donors to help him fund an orphanage. Together, consider why the author then shifts the narrative voice to the third person, talking *about* Jim? (A third-person narrator can be 'all-seeing' rather than just speaking from Jim's viewpoint.) Pause to consider what we learn about Jim. (His father has died, his mother is sick and unable to work; Jim has spent the last of their money on a pie.)

Continue reading through the next two chapters. Ask: *Why does the Stick Man throw them out?* (They haven't paid their rent.) Pause at the end of Chapter 2 to note that it is winter and snowing – making the family's plight harder as they seek somewhere to stay. Read on. Ask: *Why does Jim's Ma seek out Rosie?* (She can help Jim's sisters find work and somewhere to live.) *Why can't Jim and his mother stay?* (She is too ill and he is too young to work.) Encourage the children to consider the contrast between his lordship's house and the place where Jim has been living – the gap between the rich and poor in Victorian times.

The workhouse (Chapters 4 to 8)

Begin Chapter 4. Ask: *Do you know what a workhouse was?* (an institution where the poor, sick and homeless were sent to live to keep them off the streets) Read to the end of the chapter. Ask: *What has happened to worsen Jim's plight?* (His mother has died in the workhouse infirmary.) Read Chapter 5 and ask the children to summarise the daily routine (the cold wash, sweeping the yard, meals). Ask: *What keeps Jim going?* (the thought of escaping and finding a home)

Continue reading to the end of Chapter 7. Use the dialogue with Tip to raise question 12 on the Guided reading bookmark. Encourage the children to look for later examples. Ask: *How does Tip help Jim cope?* (He uses humour to lighten the bleak days.) Ask question 1 on the bookmark. *What is the 'hook' that makes us want to read on at the end of Chapter 7?* (to find out if and how Jim will escape) Read Chapter 8. Ask: *How does Jim escape?* (The man who comes to pick up the carpets leaves the gate open and is distracted by the workhouse woman.) Pause to notice the impact of the final short sentence at the end of Chapter 8.

Street life (Chapters 9 to 12)

Read Chapter 9. Ask: *What do we learn about the boy Jim encounters?* (He sweeps the streets to earn coins from passers-by.) Carry on reading through Chapter 10. Ask: *Why are Rosie and Judd no longer there?* (They were dismissed by his lordship for harbouring Jim's sisters.) Point out that Lame Betsy is also scratching a living but that Jim hopes he can work for her and find the thing he most wants – a home. Read to the end of the chapter and check that the children understand why Jim cries when Rosie hugs him (her affection brings out all his pent-up grief for his mother who died in the infirmary).

Read the first few paragraphs of Chapter 11. Ask: *What does the river (Thames) represent to Jim?* (the big wide world, travel, freedom) Read to the end of the chapter. Ask the children if they think the story Rosie tells Jim about his sisters is true, or might she have made it up, and if so why? (She tells a white lie to try to reassure him that his sisters are safe and happy.) Begin reading Chapter 12, pausing at Betsy's description of the doctor. Ask: *Who do you think this is?* (Dr Barnardo) Link to question 16 on the bookmark. Read on to the end of the chapter. Ask: *How does Shrimps survive?* (selling bootlaces on the streets) *What do we learn about his mother?* (She takes money from him to buy gin.) Focus on the beginning of the chapter and the last part, discussing how it emphasises the contrast between Jim's contented sleep after finding a brother in Shrimps, and the sudden shock of Rosie's grandfather discovering him and selling him to Grimy Nick. What do the children deduce from this 'sale'? (that Jim is being sold to work for Nick)

The *Lily* (Chapters 13 to 18)

Read Chapter 13. Use the descriptions of the *Lily* and the river to raise question 10 on the bookmark, again encouraging the children to look out for further examples. Ask: *What is Nick forcing Jim to do?* (help unload coal from the boat into a basket) Ask: *Why was coal so important in Victorian times?* (It was used to heat homes and also power trains and machinery.) *How would the children describe the work Jim has to do? What makes the job worse?* (Nick is cruel and nasty; he has a dangerous dog called Snipe.)

Begin reading Chapter 14, pausing to ask question 11 on the bookmark. If necessary, define anthropomorphism (a literary device which sees human characteristics in something which is not human). Continue reading to the end of the chapter. Ask: *What gives Jim unusual 'bravado'?* (He has been drinking beer.) *What dream of Jim's comes true at the end of the chapter?* (The boat is on the move; they are going downstream.) Read on through Chapter 15. Pause to consider questions 2 and 3 on the bookmark. Reflect on the mood at the end of this chapter (It seems bleak and hopeless.) Ask: *What is Jim still seeking when he asks Josh if he can join him?* (a home) Elicit that this is a recurring quest in Jim's adventure which will only be resolved if he can find a safe and happy home.

Read the first part of Chapter 16, as far as 'Just pretend he ain't there at all.' Ask: *What has Nick shown Jim?* (that he is a cruel master who has only brought him scraps of food, although he himself has eaten well) Ask: *What changes in the way Jim behaves towards Nick now?* (He does not speak to him.) Consider question 4 on the bookmark. Finish the chapter and read Chapter 17 as far as 'One day, Nick. You'll be sorry you did this to me.' Ask: *What has made things worse for Jim?* (He has a bad leg injury and Nick has now tied him up with a rope so he cannot escape.) Consider how Jim's words are a hook, encouraging us to keep reading to find out if and how he can get his revenge on Grimy Nick.

Continue reading to the end of the chapter and pause to ask: *What do we learn about Jim from this episode?* (Although Nick is cruel to him, the boy saves his life.) Read Chapter 18 at pace. Ask: *How does Jim plan his escape?* (He uses sharp coal to cut the rope around his neck, then ties up Snipe and waits for Nick to get drunk, then uses heavy coal to weigh down the hatch, trapping Nick inside.) Ask: *What keeps Jim going and encourages him?* (the voice inside his head, which is like having a brother alongside him) Again, note the short sentence at the end of the chapter as Jim becomes free.

The circus (Chapters 19 to 21)

Read at pace through Chapter 19 and begin Chapter 20 as far as 'He gazed at the little van, and his old longing rose up in him again'. Ask: *What is it that Jim most longs for?* (a home) Read the next two chapters, pausing in the final paragraph to raise question 5 on the bookmark. Highlight the sudden change in mood again, from hope and excitement at finding a home in the circus to the realisation that he has once again been sold for a coin. Remind the children of the first time Rosie's grandfather sold him.

Back on the streets (Chapters 22 to 24)

Continue reading. Pause to ask: *How does Jim's inner voice or 'bruvver' give him encouragement and keep him going?* (For example, it tells him that the lane must lead somewhere; it reminds him that Rosie will be in London.) Ask: *Do you think Jim would have stolen food at the beginning of the story? What has changed?* (He has had to learn to fend for himself; he is frightened that adults will betray him again to Nick.) Raise question 6 on the bookmark. Read at pace Chapters 23 and 24. Ask: *What does Jim think is wrong with Shrimps at first?* (He is afraid that Shrimps might have cholera.) Explain that diseases like typhoid and cholera were rife in Victorian London because of the living conditions of the poor. Link to question 13 on the bookmark. What does Shrimps say is actually wrong with him? (He was beaten up and knocked out by some men who thought he'd stolen money from an old man.)

Home at last (Chapters 25 to 27)

Read Chapter 25. Pause to ask the children to recall the first time Jim sees the doctor (when Betsy takes him to hear the doctor speak). Explain that Barnardo was not a doctor, but people referred to him as 'Doctor' so Jim thinks he can help save Shrimps. Ask: *What do we learn at the end of the chapter, in another very short, punchy sentence?* (that it is too late: Shrimps has died) Continue reading to the end of the novel. Focus on the last sentence. Ask: *How is this a resolution of Jim's quest?* (He has finally found the thing he most wanted: a home.) Consider questions 14 and 17 on the bookmark. Together read the author's note and reflect on the way the author has based a fictional story on historical fact. Looking back on the novel as a whole, discuss questions 7 to 9 and 15 on the bookmark.

Street Child
by Berlie Doherty

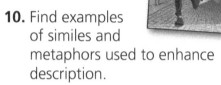

Focus on...
Meaning

1. What is the 'wild thing' that Jim feels fluttering inside him?

2. Jim looks forward to his first trip on the *Lily* – why? How does it really turn out?

3. Explain what Josh tells Jim about his soul.

4. How does Jim create a 'bruvver' for himself? Who inspires it?

5. What is the thing that Jim 'never thought to see again in his life'?

6. Which words best describe Jim's character? What are his skills and strengths?

Focus on...
Organisation

7. Jim's adventure has several episodes/settings – can you identify them?

8. What are the key turning points in the narrative?

9. How much do the chapter headings tell us?

Street Child
by Berlie Doherty

Focus on...
Language and features

10. Find examples of similes and metaphors used to enhance description.

11. The author uses anthropomorphism to describe the river and other features. What effect does this have?

12. Find words or spellings that the author invents to represent the street children's language.

13. What do we learn from the novel about London in Victorian times?

Focus on...
Purpose, viewpoints and effects

14. Why do you think the author frames the first and last chapters in the first person? Why do you think she uses the third person for the rest of the narrative?

15. Identify three good characters and three nasty characters.

16. Who is the character called Barnie based on? What do you think his purpose or goal was?

17. Describe the mood or tone of the novel? Does the ending change the mood? If so, how?

SHARED READING ▶

Extract 1

- Read Extract 1. Ask: *Why is Jim excited?* (He has enough money to buy the family a meat pie.) *Why does Mrs Hodder order him out of her shop?* (She has been bothered all day by boys begging for pies and assumes Jim has no money to buy one.) *Why do the boys chase Jim?* (They are hungry and have no money so they would try to steal the pie.)

- Tell the children that they are going to focus on the descriptive writing. Ask them to identify some adjectives and underline them ('muddy', 'swaying', 'hungry', 'hot', 'soggy').

- Highlight on the extract the way the author uses active verbs to create a sense of hurry and excitement ('flung', 'dodged'). Circle the verb 'prised' and ask the children if they can explain it. Ask: *Can you suggest replacements?* (forced, pulled hard) Underline the phrase 'slithered and skidded'. Point out how the author uses alliteration and also onomatopoeia, as the repeated 's' sound suggests the sliding of the horses' hooves on the snow.

- Challenge the children to identify three similes ('as hot as a piece of coal', 'winked at her like an eye', 'rock like a ship at sea'). Underline the idiom 'blue with cold'. Ask: *What does it suggest?* (extremely cold, his feet are losing blood supply because they are so cold)

- Point out that the author uses words to describe different senses: for example sight ('glowed yellow'), hearing ('gurgling'), smell ('hot gravy'), touch ('warming him through its cloth wrapping').

Extract 2

- Read Extract 2. Ask: *What time of day is it?* (morning) Focus on the descriptive language. Ask: *How does the author use personification?* (the river is described as a living thing that breathes; the boats as blooming into life) *What are the dark looming shapes?* (the boats and ships)

- Circle the noun 'gleam' and ask the children what it means (a bright light reflected from something). Point out how the author has used the noun in a metaphor to describe light reflecting on the water.

- Underline the phrases 'the knot of the *Lily*' and 'the floating castles' and ask the children to explain them. (The knot is in the rope around the *Lily*'s mooring and castle is a technical term for the area above a ship's main deck). Circle or underline any other tricky vocabulary such as 'brazier' and check that the children understand the meaning.

- Focus on the devices used to convey the character of Nick. Circle verbs ('lumbered', 'belched'). Ask: *What impression do the words give of Nick?* (He is heavy, clumsy, rude.)

- Look at the last sentence of dialogue. Ask: *What is wrong with the way Nick uses verbs?* (He uses singular forms of verbs for plural 'we.') *Can you identify which sentence is incomplete?* ('Not while there's coal in the ground.')

- Ask a volunteer to correct Nick's grammar. ("When we clear this lot, we go out for more, from one of those big boats. So don't think your work's done. Your work is never done, not while there's coal in the ground.")

Extract 3

- Read Extract 3. Ask: *What is happening?* (Jim is running away from Nick and Snipe.) *How would you describe the pace and tone of the extract?* (The narrative is fast-paced and tense.)

- Circle any tricky words and check that the children understand their meaning ('hollered', 'pummelled', 'loped'). Underline the phrase 'sent up their clamour'. Ask: *Can you suggest a replacement?* (made a lot of noise)

- Together, examine the devices the author uses to create pace and excitement. Highlight the short, snappy sentences with strong active verbs. Underline all the verbs that describe running/ movement – 'sprinted', 'dodging', 'run', 'loped', 'flung'. Ask: *Can you think of any other verbs that the author could have used?* (race, rush, dash, dart, shot, flew) Reflect how repeating the same verb (ran/running) would have made the narrative repetitive and less lively.

- Ask the children to think about which sense the author concentrates on in this passage (hearing/ sound). Challenge them to identify all the words and phrases describing sound ('howls', 'hollered', 'clamour', 'hear', 'breathing', 'flapping', 'snapped', 'rustling', 'snuffling', 'panting'). Read 'everything had gone silent again'. Ask: *What effect does this have?* (It increases the tension as Jim is expecting Snipe to spring.)

- Focus on the phrase 'the voice crept into his head'. Can the children explain what the voice is? (the inner voice that encourages Jim on, like a brother)

- Ask: *What effect do the questions at the end of the extract have?* (They create suspense.) *What is Jim frightened of?* (He may have murdered Nick.)

Extract 4

- Read aloud the title of Extract 4. Ask: *Can you suggest what it means?* (that coal was all-important to the Victorians) *Can you explain the link to a familiar old nursery rhyme?* ('Old King Cole')

- Check that the children know when the Victorian age was. (Queen Victoria's reign was from 1837 to 1901.)

- Underline tricky words or phrases ('fossil fuel', 'ventilate', 'merchants', 'sulphurous', 'billowed', 'belched', 'polluted', 'respiratory'). In each case, ask the children if they can explain the meaning of the word and suggest replacement words or phrases.

- Focus on 'fossil fuel fed' and note the alliteration. Ask: *Can you identify any other alliterative phrases?* ('billowed and belched')

- Consider how the information in the extract links back to the novel. Ask: *Which job do Nick and Jim do?* (They work as coal backers.) *What sort of vessel is the* Lily? (a coal lighter) *Can you remember which job Josh does?* (He works on one of the coal ships that bring coal down from the North to be transferred to the coal lighters.) Point out the reference to children working in the mines and tell the children that until laws were passed during the Victorian age, even small children were made to work 12-hour days in the coal mines.

- Focus on the description of the pollution caused by burning coal and remind the children of the author's evocative descriptions of fog on the river. Tell them that dangerous smogs continued in London up until the 1950s when new laws were passed to clean up the air.

Extract 1

Jim Jarvis hopped about on the edge of the road, his feet blue with cold. Passing carriages flung muddy snow up into his face and his eyes, and the swaying horses slithered and skidded as they were whipped on by their drivers. At last Jim saw his chance and made a dash for it through the traffic. The little shops in the dark street all glowed yellow with their hanging lamps, and Jim dodged from one light to the next until he came to the shop he was looking for. It was the meat pudding shop. Hungry boys and skinny dogs hovered round the doorway, watching for scraps. Jim pushed past them, his coin as hot as a piece of coal in his fist. He could hear his stomach gurgling as the rich smell of hot gravy met him.

Mrs Hodder was trying to sweep the soggy floor and sprinkle new straw down when Jim ran in.

"You can run right out again," she shouted to him. "If I'm not sick of little boys today!"

"But I've come to buy a pudding!" Jim told her. He danced up and down, opening and closing his fist so his coin winked at her like an eye.

She prised it out of his hand and bit it. "Where did you find this, little shrimp?" she asked him. "And stop your dancing! You're making me rock like a ship at sea!"

Jim hopped on to a dry patch of straw. "Ma's purse. And she said there won't be no more, because that's the last shilling we got, and I know that's true because I emptied it for her. So make it a good one, Mrs Hodder. Make it big, and lots of gravy!"

He ran home with the pie clutched to his chest, warming him through its cloth wrapping. Some of the boys outside the shop tried to chase him, but he soon lost them in the dark alleys, his heart thudding in case they caught him and stole the pie.

Extract 2

Jim woke up before Grimy Nick. The river was overflowing with mist and seemed to be breathing with secrets, with dark looming shapes. When the mist began to lift they bloomed into life, like a city, street upon street of boats. He could see downriver to the long silver gleam of water, under the dark arches of a bridge, and he knew that far away from there it flowed out to the sea. He imagined slipping the knot of the *Lily* and drifting downstream with her past all the floating castles of tall sailing ships and out to the huge ocean.

When Grimy Nick lumbered up from his dark hole he swore at Jim for letting the fire in the brazier go out. "You'd think we didn't have any coal on board, you fool." He laughed at his own joke, a great startling whoop of laughter that set Snipe leaping up out of his sleep. Jim tried to laugh with him.

"Get water from the yard," Nick snarled. "Start the day off right."

When Jim came back with his slopping pail he found Nick toasting fish by the fire. He threw a piece in one direction for Jim and some heads in another direction for the dog. Then he wiped his mouth with the back of his hand and belched.

"Work!" he told Jim. "When we clears this lot, we goes out for more, off one of them big boats. So don't think yer work's done. Yer work's never done. Not while there's coal in the ground."

Extract 3

Instantly Snipe was awake. His howls rang across the night. He strained to pull against the rope, in a fury to be free. Grimy Nick hollered himself into wakefulness and pummelled his fists against the hatch. Across the fields all the backyard animals sent up their clamour. Lights blazed across the water.

Jim sprinted on steadily, head down, dodging between bushes and trees. He could hear his own breathing, and the flapping of his boot soles. Brambles tore at his breeches and his jacket. An overhanging branch snapped at his cap and held it trapped, and Jim had to run back and tear it free. He loped on, his chest tight and bursting, his legs as heavy as lead weights. He had no idea where he was going.

He heard rustling in the undergrowth behind him and knew he that he was being followed. The rustling became a snuffling and panting. It was a dog. Jim's leg hurt so much now that he couldn't run any further. In total weariness he flung himself down, head-first, covered his face with his hands, and waited for Snipe to spring.

He was aware that everything had gone silent again, as if the world had sunk back into sleep. At last he made himself turn his head. The dog was not Snipe at all, but a small terrier. He licked Jim's outstretched hand and ran away again through a hedge. There wasn't a sound. If Snipe still howled, he couldn't be heard from here. If Nick still hammered and swore then the noise he made was lost in the night.

"What if they're dead, bruvver?" the voice crept into his head. "What if old Nick's suffocating down there in the hold? What if Snipe's strangled himself on that rope?" He sat up, drenched with cold sweat. "What if you've killed them?"

Extract 4

King Coal by Jillian Powell

Coal was king in the Victorian age. The fossil fuel fed the steam engines that powered locomotives, ships and factory machinery and heated homes, shops and offices. Every year, millions of tons of coal were transported from the coalfields of the North of England to London by rail and sea. The industry employed an army of workers, from the miners who hacked at the coalface in mines with hand picks and shovels, to the children who worked as hurriers pulling heavy carts of coal on chains around their waists, or trappers who sat for twelve hours a day in darkness, opening and closing doors to ventilate the tunnels. Workers were also needed to transport the coal from incoming ships to coal cellars in the city. Whippers carried sacks onto the coal merchants' lighters; backers transferred it onshore; sifters sorted it and fillers filled the sacks which were loaded onto waggons and delivered by trimmers.

The thick, sulphurous smoke that billowed and belched from chimneys drowned the city in dense smog. The soot that drifted down was called 'blacks', as it coated everything in fine, black coal dust. In damp weather, the smoke combined with fog to form a dense, dangerous smog also known as a pea-souper. At times, the fog was so thick that horse-drawn carts and coaches had to be led by men carrying torches. Along the River Thames, where it was often worst, steamers had to wait for it to lift before they could start their journeys. There were frequent accidents, from people falling into the Thames to coal barges running into bridges and sinking, and horses and carts overturning. The murky, polluted air also caused lung diseases and respiratory illnesses. This deadly mixture of soot, smoke and fog became known as a 'London particular'.

GRAMMAR, PUNCTUATION & SPELLING ▶

1. Not just nouns

> **Objective**
> To use expanded noun phrases to convey complicated information concisely.
>
> **What you need**
> Copies of *Street Child*, Extract 1, photocopiable page 22 'Not just nouns'.

What to do

- Display an enlarged copy of Extract 1. Re-read the extract together, then circle the words 'horses', 'street', and 'floor'. Ask*: Can you identify what part of speech they are?* (nouns) Examine the phrases which expand the nouns to describe them further: 'the swaying horses', 'the dark street', 'the soggy floor'.

- Tell the children that we call this kind of phrase an expanded noun phrase. It is a neat, concise way of conveying more about the noun. Challenge them to find more expanded noun phrases in the extract, underlining or circling them ('Passing carriages', 'the meat pudding shop', 'a dry patch of straw'). Note how the phrase gives us more information about the noun in each case. Ask: *Can you suggest other adjectives that could expand the phrases further?* (For example, the nervous, swaying horses; the dark, narrow street; the tempting meat pudding shop.)

- Arrange the children into pairs and hand out photocopiable page 22 'Not just nouns'. Allow them time to fill it in then bring the class back together to review their work.

> **Differentiation**
> **Support:** Provide a list of adjectives to help children compose phrases.
> ___
> **Extension:** Challenge the children to write more noun phrases and sentences for other nouns taken from the novel.

2. Verb switch

> **Objective**
> To use passive verbs to affect the presentation of information in a sentence.
>
> **What you need**
> Copies of *Street Child*, photocopiable page 23 'Verb switch'.

What to do

- Write these two sentences on the board: 'Rosie rocked Jim to sleep.' and 'Jim was rocked to sleep by Rosie.'

- Underline the passive and active verbs. Ask: *What difference does the verb form make to the sense or meaning of the sentence?* (The passive puts the emphasis on Jim; the active on Rosie.) Challenge volunteers to suggest follow-on sentences, retaining the same subject but using a pronoun to avoid repetition, for example: 'Jim was rescued by Barnie. He was living on the streets.'; 'Barnie rescued Jim. He gave him a home.'

- Hand out photocopiable page 23 'Verb switch'. Allow the children time to read through and fill in the sheet, working individually or in pairs.

- When they have finished, ask volunteers to read aloud all the sentences on the sheet which use a passive verb. Reflect how this puts all the emphasis on the character of Jim and what happened to him in the story. Repeat the exercise asking volunteers to read aloud all the sentences which use the active form. Reflect how the emphasis has now switched to the other characters and how they treated Jim.

> **Differentiation**
> **Support:** Before they begin, model several short sentences on the board in both forms.
> ___
> **Extension:** Ask pairs to rewrite all the sentences using the passive form in the first person as if Jim is speaking to them. (For example, 'I was sold by Rosie's grandfather.')

3. Perfect verbs

Objective

To use the perfect form of verbs to mark relationships of time and cause.

What you need

Copies of *Street Child*, Extract 1.

What to do

- Display Extract 1 to establish that the main narrative is in the simple past tense. Explain that the author uses different verb tenses at different times to achieve effects, for example, 'Tell Me Your Story, Jim' is written in the present tense, as if Jim is talking to us in the here and now. 'Here I am with food in my belly' is also written in the present tense. At other times, the author uses the perfect form of the verb when talking about something in the past which is still happening. For example, when Jim says at the workhouse 'I've been here a year.' Write this quote on the board and ask the children to expand the abbreviated form: 'I have been here a year.'

- Arrange the children into pairs. Tell them to imagine that Barnie interviews Jim at earlier times in the story. Together, list on the board key times in his life: in the workhouse, helping Rosie as Skipping Jim, working on the coal lighter, working at the circus, living rough on the streets/looking after Shrimps.

- They should practise the present-perfect form by taking turns to ask/answer the question: 'How long have you been/worked…?' Before they begin, they should skim and scan the novel for clues for information that Jim would tell Barnie.

Differentiation

Support: Provide chapter references to help children find relevant clues (Chapters 4 to 7; 12; 13 to 18; 21; 23 to 27).

Extension: Encourage them to brainstorm further questions and expand their answers, for example, using 'since', 'before'.

4. Modals

Objective

To use and understand modal verbs.

What you need

Copies of *Street Child*.

What to do

- Ask: *What is Jim searching for throughout the novel?* (a home) Suggest that, at times, he thinks or hopes he has found one. Let the children work in pairs to find examples to support this, such as when Jim thinks he could work for Betsy, or Rosie; when he has the idea of going with Josh; working at Juglini's Circus.

- Bring the class back together and note their ideas on the board. Ask: *What did Jim think or hope could happen?* Highlight the modal verb: 'could'. On the board list: 'can', 'could', 'may', 'might', 'shall', 'should', 'will', 'would', 'must'. Tell the children that we use these verbs (modals) to indicate things that are possible or to suggest how likely they are to happen.

- Write on the board: 'Jim hopes he _____ stay with Rosie.' and 'Jim hoped he _____ stay with Rosie.' Note the verb tenses and ask the children to suggest modal verbs to fill the gaps ('can'/'may'/'will'; 'could'/'might'/'would').

- In their pairs, tell children to draft pairs of sentences about Jim's hopes using the present and past tense, trying out different modals (for example, 'Jim thinks he may be able to go with Josh.'; 'Jim thought he might be able to go with Josh.') Encourage them to discuss their choices. Ask: *Which tense makes it sound more/less likely?*

Differentiation

Support: Let pairs focus on one pair of modals, such as 'can'/'could' or 'may'/'might'.

Extension: Encourage children to try out as many modal verbs as possible.

5. How many homophones?

Objective
To distinguish between homophones and other words which are often confused.

What you need
Copies of *Street Child,* Extract 2.

What to do

- Display Extract 2. Tell the children that they are going to try to identify all the words in the extract which have homophones, writing down the word and its homophone to show the difference in spelling. Demonstrate by circling the word 'mist' and asking a volunteer to suggest its homophone (missed). Challenge them to use the homophone in a sentence about the novel to bring out its meaning ('Jim missed his mother and sisters.')

- Arrange the class into pairs and tell them to work through the whole extract, finding and writing down as many words as they can which have homophones.

- When they have compiled a list of words and their homophones, they should draft a pair of short sentences about Jim or a topic from the novel, using the word and its homophone to show the differences in spelling and meaning.

- Bring the class back together and compile a list of words from the extract on the board: 'mist', 'see', 'knew', 'there', 'knot', 'past', 'hole', 'board', 'great', 'right', 'pail', 'by', 'threw', 'piece'.

- Invite paired volunteers to read their sentences and spell the two homophones ('missed', 'sea', 'new', 'their', 'not', 'passed', 'whole', 'bored', 'grate', 'write', 'pale', 'buy', 'through', 'peace'.) Encourage the class to give feedback on which sentences work best and which were the trickiest homophones to find/write sentences for.

Differentiation
Support: Limit the task to finding the words and their homophones, sharing their spellings and meanings as a class.

Extension: Encourage pairs to skim and scan a chapter of the novel to repeat the exercise.

6. Silent letters

Objective
To spell some words with 'silent' letters.

What you need
Copies of *Street Child*, photocopiable page 24 'Silent letters'.

What to do

- Refer to the author's note at the end of the novel in which she describes how meeting the real Jim Jarvis made Dr Barnardo aware of the 'plight of destitute children in London'. Write on the board the word 'plight'. Ask: *Can you provide a definition of the word 'plight'?* (dangerous, difficult or unfortunate situation) Examine the spelling, circling the silent letters 'gh'. Can the children suggest any other words with a similar sound or spelling? ('light', 'bright', 'flight', 'fright' and so on)

- Challenge them to suggest ways to help them memorise the spelling, focusing on the silent letters.

- Tell the children that they are going to do a spelling task based on tricky words with silent letters taken from the novel. Arrange them into pairs and hand out photocopiable page 24 'Silent letters'. Allow them time to complete the activity then bring the class back together to discuss their answers, writing them on the board and circling the silent letters.

- Let pairs take a closer look at the spellings, working with their partner to try to devise ways to help them remember the spellings, for example, by sounding aloud silent letters, creating a mnemonic, writing those letters in capitals or underlining or circling them.

Differentiation
Support: Provide the context of the word from the novel.

Extension: Let pairs work together, choosing a word at a time, to draft sentences about characters or subjects in the novel.

Not just nouns

● Write an expanded noun phrase for each noun taken from the novel. Then use it in a complete sentence.

1. River

Noun phrase: _____

Sentence: _____

_____

2. Coal

Noun phrase: _____

Sentence: _____

_____

3. Boat

Noun phrase: _____

Sentence: _____

_____

4. Dog

Noun phrase: _____

Sentence: _____

_____

5. Caravan

Noun phrase: _____

Sentence: _____

_____

6. Circus

Noun phrase: _____

Sentence: _____

_____

Verb switch

● Read the following sentences. Write A or P in the second column to show if the verb is active (A) or passive (P). Then rewrite each sentence in the third column, switching the verb form.

Jim was sold by Rosie's grandfather.		
Mr Barrack caned Jim.		
Grimy Nick treated Jim cruelly.		
Jim was bitten by Snipe.		
The cry of a cockerel woke Jim.		
Jim was given a home by Barnie.		

● Write your own active sentence related to Street Child and then write the same sentence in the passive form.

Active sentence	**Passive sentence**

GRAMMAR, PUNCTUATION & SPELLING

Silent letters

- Match the words in the boxes to the correct dictionary definitions in the table. Write each word in the correct space and circle the silent letters in each word.

plight	jostled	wharf	lighter	autumn	cholera	ache

Word	Meaning
	dangerous, difficult or unfortunate situation
	large, flat-bottomed vessels for carrying coal and other goods
	a harbour structure for mooring boats
	a disease caused by dirty water
	a season that falls between summer and winter
	a continuous, dull pain
	pushed and shoved

PLOT, CHARACTER & SETTING ▶

1. Jim's journey

Objectives
To identify and discuss themes and conventions in a wide range of writing; to make comparisons across books.

What you need
Copies of *Street Child*, photocopiable page 29 'Jim's journey'.

What to do

- Ask: *Which genre(s) do you think the novel fits into and why?* (an historical novel because it is set in the past; an adventure story because Jim is on a type of journey or quest) Tell the children that they are going to focus on how far the plot fits into a classic adventure story.

- Begin by brainstorming together some typical features of an adventure story, encouraging children to cite other novels or films as examples (a likeable hero or heroine, a quest or journey, dangers to be faced). List their ideas on the board.

- Arrange the children into pairs and hand out photocopiable page 29 'Jim's journey'. Allow them time to fill it in, referring to the novel for evidence or information.

- Bring the class back together and discuss how far the novel is a classic adventure story and in what ways it deviates (for example, adventure stories often have exotic or unusual settings, whereas *Street Child* is set in a real, historical past). Reflect that novels often fit into more than one genre.

Differentiation
Extension: Encourage pairs to use the photocopiable page to explore other adventure stories, comparing and contrasting them with the novel.

2. Just Jim

Objective
To articulate and justify arguments and opinions.

What you need
Copies of *Street Child*.

What to do

- Tell the children that they are going to focus on Jim Jarvis. Ask: *Can you think of any adjectives to describe Jim's character?* Encourage volunteers to suggest a word to describe Jim, backing it up with a reason or explanation (for example, Jim is lonely because he wishes he had a brother; Jim is clever because he gets away from Grimy Nick; Jim is kind because he looks after Shrimps when he is sick).

- Arrange the children into pairs and allow them time to think of at least three adjectives that they think best describe Jim, using evidence from the novel. They should write down their ideas. When they have finished, bring the class back together to share their ideas.

- Ask: *Which qualities make him a likeable hero?* (his bravery, kindness) *Which qualities make him vulnerable?* (being young and alone) Focusing on the words the children have used, encourage discussion of how his character helps shape the story (for example, he has to be brave to run away from the workhouse, or escape from Grimy Nick; being young and alone puts him at the mercy of cruel people like Nick).

Differentiation
Support: Provide a list of adjectives for the children to choose from ('brave', 'kind', 'lonely', 'clever', 'hard-working', 'strong', 'tough' and so on).

3. Recognising moods

Objective
To explain and discuss their understanding of what they have read.

What you need
Copies of *Street Child*, photocopiable page 30 'Jim's destiny'.

Cross-curricular link
PSHE

What to do

- Ask: *Why does Jim find himself alone on his adventure?* (His mother dies, making him an orphan, and he is separated from his sisters.) Suggest that authors often use orphans as their lead character as this allows them freedom in what happens. It also means that they have to face challenges alone. As an orphan and a child, Jim is at the mercy of the other characters, good or bad, he encounters.

- Tell the children that they are going to think about how other characters in the novel directly shape Jim's destiny. Ask a volunteer to suggest one character who directly affects Jim's destiny and explain how (for example, Rosie's grandfather, by selling him to Grimy Nick).

- Arrange the children into pairs and hand out photocopiable page 30 'Jim's destiny'. Allow the children time to consider each character then bring the class back together to share their findings. Ask: *In what ways do you think Jim decides his own destiny? What helps him?* (his resilience, spirit, determination) *What hinders him?* (Victorian society, which allows children to be used as work slaves)

Differentiation
Support: As a class, discuss one character on photocopiable page 30 before pairs begin work.

Extension: Encourage children to compare other novels with orphan lead characters and identify which qualities they share.

4. Novel geography

Objective
To retrieve, record and present information from non-fiction.

What you need
Copies of *Street Child*.

Cross-curricular link
Geography

What to do

- Tell the children that they are going to focus on descriptions of London in the novel. Ask: *Can you remember any places or landmarks in London that feature in the novel?* (the statue of a man on a horse, the River Thames, the wharves)

- Arrange the children into small groups and assign them three or four chapters each. Tell the children to skim and scan their chapters for any information about London. They can include buildings, streets, landmarks and features. They should nominate a note taker to make brief notes as they work.

- Bring the class back together to collate ideas on the board. These could include the River Thames, the wharves, tree-lined streets with grand houses, a statue of a man on horseback, a fountain and so on. Allow groups time to do some research on the Internet to find features like those described in the novel, searching for statues of a man on a horse, a fountain (as in Trafalgar Square), the River Thames and so on. Again, let them take brief notes, then bring the class back together and ask volunteers to share their findings.

Differentiation
Support: Let groups focus their research on one feature or landmark such as the River Thames or the statue of a man on a horse.

Extension: Groups can use their notes to write a London glossary, linking descriptions in the novel to real features and places.

5. The workhouse

Objective
To summarise the main ideas drawn from more than one paragraph, identifying key details that support the main ideas.

What you need
Copies of *Street Child*, photocopiable page 31 'The workhouse'.

Cross-curricular link
History

What to do
- Ask: *Where is the story set? And when?* (London in the 1860s) Remind the children that within the setting are descriptions of a workhouse, a coal lighter on the Thames and a travelling circus. Explain that they are going to focus on the workhouse.

- Check that the children understand what a workhouse was (an institution where people without jobs or homes were sent to live and work in Victorian times). Workhouses housed orphans, the sick, disabled, elderly and unmarried mothers. Explain that there was no welfare support as there is now. People were expected to earn their keep by doing jobs in the workhouse. Ask: *How do the characters see the workhouse in the novel?* (They fear and dread it.) *Why do you think it was so feared?* (Families were split up, living conditions were hard and bleak, it felt like a prison.)

- Arrange the children into pairs and hand out photocopiable page 31 'The workhouse'. Tell them to scan Chapters 4 to 8 for information to help them fill it in. Allow them time to complete the sheet then bring the class back together to share their findings.

Differentiation
Support: Give children some key words for each heading to help them write their sentences.

Extension: Let children use books or the Internet to find out more about Victorian workhouses to add to their sheets.

6. Grimy Nick

Objective
To draw inferences, such as inferring characters' feelings, thoughts and motives from their actions, and justifying inferences with evidence.

What you need
Copies of *Street Child*.

What to do
- Begin by suggesting that in any adventure story, the hero or heroine is likely to encounter good and bad characters. Ask: *Can you suggest characters that Jim encounters that are either nice or nasty?* (Rosie, Tip, Shrimps, Barnie are nice; the Stick Man, Mr Barrack, Rosie's grandfather, Grimy Nick are nasty.)

- Tell the children that they are going to focus on perhaps the nastiest villain in the plot: Grimy Nick. Brainstorm some words which best describe Nick ('cruel', 'hard', 'dirty', 'tough', 'selfish').

- Write on the board three headings: 'Appearance', 'Behaviour/actions', 'Dialogue'. Explain that they are going to explore how the author uses these to convey character.

- Arrange the children into pairs. Tell them to scan Chapters 12 to 21 and find the best examples they can for each of the three categories, writing down examples of descriptions of Nick's appearance, behaviour and actions, and also examples of things he says that convey his character.

- When they have finished, bring the class back together to share their findings. Reflect how Nick's character is conveyed by his abrupt, ungrammatical speech, as well as words and phrases used to describe him and his behaviour.

Differentiation
Support: Find some examples for each heading and write them on the board before pairs begin.

Extension: Let pairs use their notes to describe Nick in Jim's words.

7. Plot markers

Objective

To explain and discuss their understanding of what they have read.

What you need

Copies of *Street Child*.

Cross-curricular link

PSHE

What to do

- Suggest that adventure stories need ups and downs in the plot, times when the hero or heroine feels happy or hopeful, sad or afraid. Ask for volunteers to cite emotions that Jim feels during the story and write their suggestions on the board (sad, scared, worried, excited). Ask: *What was happening to Jim to make him feel that way?* (He felt sad when his mother died, he felt scared when he went in the workhouse and so on.)

- Suggest that his emotions reflect twists and turns in the plot: when he is working for Rosie Jim feels happy, but then there is a turn in the plot when Rosie's grandfather discovers him and sells him to Nick, and Jim feels upset and afraid.

- Arrange the children into pairs. Tell them to list the emotions Jim feels during the story, linking them to events (for example, he feels happy when he buys the meat pie for his family. He feels excited when the *Lily* heads towards the sea).

- Bring the class back together. Ask volunteers to suggest which emotions are markers for significant developments in the plot, collating their ideas on the board.

Differentiation

Support: Let pairs list emotions that Jim feels during the story. Ask them to concentrate on two emotions and find examples in the story.

Extension: Encourage pairs to explore other markers in plot development, such as changes of location.

8. Plot predictions

Objective

To predict what might happen from details stated and implied.

What you need

Copies of *Street Child*.

What to do

- Tell the children that they are going to look at devices the author uses to keep the reader engaged and wanting to find out what happens next. Suggest that authors often use chapter ends to raise questions that we might want answered. Look together at the last lines of Chapter 5, where Jim dreams of escaping, to demonstrate this. Ask: *What can we predict will happen?* (He will try to escape from the workhouse.) *What questions does this leave unanswered?* (How will he manage to escape? Will he find a safe home, and if so where and how?)

- Arrange the children into small groups and assign them four or five chapters each. Tell them to examine the chapter endings. Ask: *What can we predict will happen? What questions are left unanswered?* Groups should appoint a note taker to write down their ideas as they work.

- When they have scanned all their chapters, encourage them to decide which chapter ends have the most significant 'hooks' to make us want to read on.

- Bring the class back together and invite volunteers from each group to share their findings. Ask: *How does the author use these hooks to keep us guessing what will happen?*

Differentiation

Support: Identify key chapters – such as 14, 18 and 21 – for groups to focus on.

Extension: Encourage the children to identify similar 'hooks' within chapters (for example, within Chapter 16).

Jim's journey

● Use your knowledge of *Street Child* to help you identify the main features of the story.

1. Name of hero or heroine. _____

2. What is the goal of their journey or quest?

_____

_____

_____

3. List three dangers or obstacles they face along the way.

    a. _____

    b. _____

    c. _____

4. Who or what helps them overcome their obstacles?

_____

_____

_____

_____

_____

5. How do they reach their goal in the end?

_____

_____

_____

_____

Jim's destiny

● What do the following characters do to change Jim's destiny?

<table>
<tr><td>

1. Jim's Ma

_____

_____

_____

_____

_____

</td><td>

2. Grimy Nick

_____

_____

_____

_____

_____

_____

</td></tr>
</table>

<table>
<tr><td>

3. Shrimps

_____

_____

_____

_____

_____

</td><td>

4. Madame Juglini

_____

_____

_____

_____

_____

</td></tr>
</table>

5. Barnie

_____

_____

_____

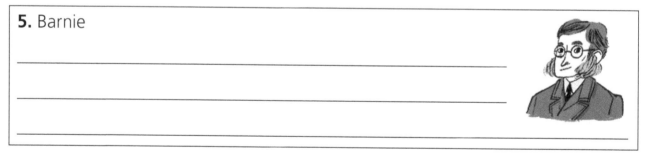

● What does Jim do to change his own destiny?

_____

_____

_____

The workhouse

● Imagine Jim is telling Shrimps about his time in the workhouse. Write a few sentences in Jim's own words. The first one has been started for you.

1. Refectory/meals

We had to queue in silence. We sat at long tables. We ate… _____

_____

2. Clothes

_____

_____

3. Sleeping arrangements

_____

_____

_____

4. School

_____

_____

_____

5. Work/jobs

_____

_____

_____

6. Infirmary

_____

_____

7. Asylum

_____

_____

TALK ABOUT IT ▶

1. Then and now

Objective
To ask questions to improve understanding.

What you need
Copies of *Street Child*.

Cross-curricular link
History

What to do

- Tell the children that they are going to discuss how Jim's life is different from theirs. Begin by describing how, in Victorian times, children born into poor families often had no education but were forced to work long hours in factories or down mines, or earn a few pennies on the streets. If they had no home or family to support them, they had to earn pennies to buy a night's shelter or they slept rough on the streets. Explain that in 1865, a journalist called Henry Mayhew wrote articles for a London newspaper about their lives and that his work, along with that of philanthropists like Dr Barnardo, helped to change attitudes and bring in new laws on child labour.

- Arrange the children into small groups. Tell them to skim and scan the novel to discuss all the things that happen to Jim and his friends that could not happen today. (For example, corporal punishment, being sold, not going to school, being made to do hard physical work, drinking ale in an alehouse.) Encourage them to think how their lives are different but also consider how some children in developing countries may still live rough or have to work rather than go to school.

Differentiation
Support: Let groups focus on four chapters then share ideas with other groups.

Extension: Challenge children to research new laws on schooling and child labour introduced during Victorian times.

2. Between the lines

Objective
To draw and justify inferences.

What you need
Copies of *Street Child*, Extract 1, photocopiable page 35 'Between the lines'.

What to do

- Read Chapter 2 as far as 'His throat filled up again.' Ask: Why does Emily tell Mr Spink that their mother is not sick? (because they want him to think she'll be able to work again and earn more money for rent) Why does Jim own up to eating pie the night before? (because he is truthful; because he is scared of Mr Spink) Ask: Do you think his sisters wanted him to tell the truth? (No, they keep quiet and Emily gives out 'a little sigh' showing she is unhappy with him.) Reflect how the author doesn't tell us these things directly, but encourages us as readers to read between the lines.

- Suggest that this happens throughout the novel and hand out photocopiable page 35 'Between the lines' for children to work through in pairs. Tell them to take turns to read each sentence then discuss with their partner what we read between the lines from what each character says.

- Bring the class back together and discuss how we read between the lines, using inference to understand characters and their motivations.

Differentiation
Support: Provide chapter references and context for the statements.

Extension: Ask pairs to scan the novel for other examples of where we need to read between the lines.

3. Fact or opinion?

Objective

To distinguish between fact and opinion.

What you need

Copies of *Street Child*, photocopiable page 36 'Fact or opinion?'

What to do

- Remind the children of the pie that Jim buys from the meat pie shop. Ask them to list everything we know about the pie, writing their suggestions on the board (for example, it cost a shilling, it is a meat pie, it is hot, it is delicious).

- Ask: *Which of your suggestions are facts about the pie and which are opinions?* Work through the list with the children, marking each one with an 'F' for fact or an 'O' for opinion (it cost a shilling – F; It is delicious – O).

- Arrange the class into small groups. Hand each group photocopiable page 36 'Fact or opinion?' Explain to the children that they should discuss and record facts we learn about each character or topic from the novel, and Jim's opinions on them. They should nominate a note-taker to list their ideas using pronouns only ('It'/'He'/'She'). For example, the workhouse: 'It is a place where people without homes and jobs go.' (F), 'It is a frightening place.' (O); Grimy Nick: 'He works on a coal lighter.' (F), 'He is a cruel master.' (O).

- When they have finished, let volunteers from each group read out their statements in random order, challenging other groups to identify the character/topic and whether each statement is fact or opinion. Reflect how facts tell us something that cannot be disputed, whereas opinions are subjective and can be challenged or opposed.

Differentiation

Support: Supply children with a list of facts and Jim's opinions. In pairs ask the children to discuss and assign each one to the correct space in the table.

Extension: Let groups extend the task by choosing their own topics or characters from the novel.

4. The voice

Objective

To develop understanding through speculating, hypothesising, imagining and exploring ideas.

What you need

Copies of *Street Child*.

Cross-curricular link

PSHE

What to do

- Together, re-read the opening of Chapter 16. Ask: *What does Jim mean when he says to himself 'You got lots of bruvvers, Jim'?* (There are many boys living as he does.) *Can you explain why this is a comfort?* (It makes him feel he is not alone.) *What prompts Jim to talk to himself?* (He has no one else to confide in.)

- Together skim and scan Chapter 16 for further examples. Notice how the words are put into speech marks, as if another person is talking. Ask: *What is the tone of the voice?* (chirpy, encouraging) *Whose voice does it echo?* (Shrimps's) Encourage the children to consider how this makes Jim feel (stronger, braver, more determined) Ask: *How do you think Jim is really feeling?* (frightened, lonely, sad) *What effect does it have on his actions?* (It encourages him to try to escape.)

- Arrange the children into small groups. Let them skim and scan Chapters 17 to 23 for further examples, discussing the effect on Jim. Ask: *Does the voice always encourage Jim or does it sometimes make him question his actions?*

- Bring the class back together and discuss how Jim has invented his own coping strategy: the sense that someone is supporting him.

Differentiation

Support: Perform the whole task as a class activity.

Extension: Let groups discuss sources of support such as confiding in family or friends, and finding others who share similar feelings.

5. Bullies all

Objective
To participate in discussions and debates.
What you need
Copies of *Street Child*.
Cross-curricular links
PSHE and Citizenship

What to do

- Invite the children to describe how Grimy Nick treats Jim. Ask: *How does he make Jim's life a misery?* (He shouts at him, makes him work long hours doing exhausting physical work, deprives him of food and ties him up with a rope.) Establish that Nick is a bully. Discuss the different forms that bullying can take, referring back to evidence in the text (mockery, shouting, physical intimidation and violence). Ask: *How does Jim cope with Nick's bullying?* (he invents a supportive voice; stops talking to Nick; plans his revenge and escape)

- Suggest that Jim, Tip and Shrimps all encounter bullies in the novel. Brainstorm some examples and list their names on the board (Mr Spink bullies Jim's family; Mr Barrack bullies Tip; Shrimps' mother bullies him and he is also attacked by a gang of bullies and so on).

- Arrange the children into small groups. Using the list on the board, let each group choose one example and discuss what form the bullying takes and the ways Jim and his friends find of coping or fighting back. Encourage them to consider why and how the bullies get away with their behaviour and whether or not the bullying depicted in the story could happen now.

Differentiation
Support: Briefly discuss each example of bullying in the novel before groups begin work.

Extension: Let groups discuss more than one example from the novel.

6. Jim's escape plan

Objective
To participate in role play and improvisations.
What you need
Copies of *Street Child*, photocopiable page 37 'Jim's escape plan'

What to do

- Ask the children to recall two occasions when Jim has to plan his escape (from the workhouse and from Grimy Nick). Ask: *Which do you think might be the most risky and scary plan? Why?* Tell them to focus on how Jim plans his escape from Grimy Nick.

- Arrange them into pairs and hand out photocopiable page 37 'Jim's escape plan'. Allow the children time to discuss and complete the sheet, re-reading Chapter 18 to help them. Bring them back together to review their work as a class. Ask: *What made Jim determined to try to escape? What were the main risks in trying to escape?* Discuss their responses. Suggest that Jim was torn: he realised he was doing something risky and dangerous but he felt impelled to try because his life with Nick was so miserable.

- Carry out a 'conscience alley' activity, with one child playing Jim and the other children standing in two rows facing each other. The child playing Jim walks between the two rows. One group should voice the reasons he must try to escape. The other should express the opposite view (that it is dangerous and risky, that he might kill Nick and become a murderer and so on).

- Let the children discuss ideas in their groups before enacting the conscience alley. Invite the child playing Jim to express how it feels being torn between the two groups and what makes him decide to try to escape.

Differentiation
Support: Re-read Chapter 18 as a shared activity before pairs begin work.

Extension: Let the children repeat the activity, focusing on Jim's escape from the workhouse.

Between the lines

What can we read 'between the lines' from what these characters say?

Tip tells Mr Barrack he was the one he heard laughing.	Rosie tells Jim his sisters are living in a summer home in the countryside.
Ma tells Jim "God help you."	Rosie tells Jim she lost her job because her cooking was so bad.
Shrimps tells Jim the crate where he lies sick is a "proper little palace".	Nick tells Jim that Snipe will be friendly to him as long as Jim is friendly to Nick.

Fact or opinion

- For each subject, write a fact we learn from the novel and Jim's opinion of it/them.

Subject	Fact	Jim's opinion
The workhouse		
Going to school		
Grimy Nick		
Rosie		
The circus		
Barnie		

Jim's escape plan

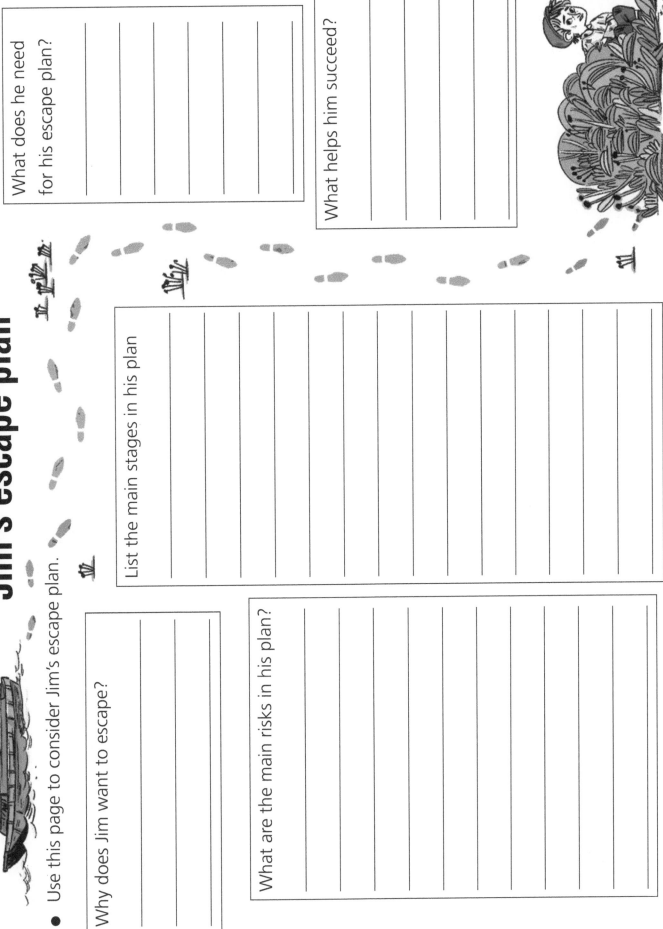

- Use this page to consider Jim's escape plan.

What does he need for his escape plan?

What helps him succeed?

List the main stages in his plan

Why does Jim want to escape?

What are the main risks in his plan?

GET WRITING ▶

1. Bang, bang

> **Objective**
> To prepare poems to perform.
> **What you need**
> Copies of *Street Child*.
> **Cross-curricular links**
> Music and drama

What to do

- Re-read the end of Chapter 6 from 'A drum was placed...' Ask: *What are Jim and Tip doing?* (They are releasing their pent-up anger by shouting out loud how they feel.) *Why can they do this without being punished?* (The noise of the music drowns out their voices.) *What effect does this have on Jim?* (He feels better for releasing his feelings.)

- Invite the children to draft a poem that Tip and Jim could sing aloud to the drums. They can include all of the things that the boys hate about the workhouse and their feelings of anger at being there. Ask them to re-read Chapters 4 to 8 for ideas (the thin gruel, the cramped sleeping boxes, the scratchy clothes).

- Brainstorm some ideas to get them started. Suggest that they could use repetition as Tip and Jim do when they repeat 'I hate this place!' Encourage them to use similes, metaphors and alliteration to help describe what the workhouse is like (dark as a dungeon; a pauper's prison).

- Let children work in pairs to draft their poem, then invite volunteers to read theirs aloud, encouraging constructive feedback.

> **Differentiation**
> **Support:** As a shared activity, brainstorm useful words and phrases and write ideas on the board.
> ___
> **Extension:** Children could set their poems or songs to simple instruments such as drums, whistles or cymbals.

2. A letter to Shrimps

> **Objective**
> To identify the audience for and purpose of the writing, selecting the appropriate form.
> **What you need**
> Copies of *Street Child*.

What to do

- Remind the children that Jim has not learned to read or write before he goes to the ragged school. Tell them that they are going to imagine that when Jim meets Josh, he persuades Josh to write a letter to Shrimps for him and makes him promise to try to find his friend to pass it on.

- Ask: *What might Jim want to tell Shrimps?* (how Rosie's grandfather sold him to Nick, who is a cruel master with a dangerous dog, Snipe; how hard the work is) List their suggestions on the board.

- Encourage them to think about how Jim might begin the letter (he might explain where and how he has met Josh) and how he might bring the letter to a close (he might tell Shrimps he will try to escape one day and come back to find him). They should skim and scan Chapters 12 to 15 for information.

- Arrange the children into pairs and allow them time to draft, edit and revise their letters. Invite volunteers to read their letters aloud to the class.

- Discuss which are the most convincing letters and why. Ask: *Which letters sound most like Jim? How would Shrimps feel reading the letter?*

> **Differentiation**
> **Support:** Re-read Chapters 12 to 15, extracting relevant information as a shared activity, before pairs begin.
> ___
> **Extension:** Pairs could try drafting a letter that Jim writes to Rosie after he has started at the ragged school.

3. Roll up, roll up!

Objective
To use organisational and presentational devices to structure text and to guide the reader.

What you need
Copies of *Street Child*, drawing materials.

Cross-curricular link
Art and design

What to do

- Tell the children that they are going to focus on the miners' pageant, which is the celecration that Jim missed out on when Nick got drunk. They are going to design a poster announcing the pageant, using all the information about it that they can find in the book.

- Before they begin working in pairs, discuss together what the poster will aim to achieve (to encourage people to come to the pageant). Brainstorm some features it will need: persuasive language, summary of main attractions (river procession, music, circus) colourful design and so on.

- Tell the children to re-read the first two pages of Chapter 18 and make notes on what they want to include. They should then sketch out a design for their poster, deciding what the main image will show and what the headline and other text will say.

- Allow them time to work on their designs and draw and colour them in. Bring the class back together and invite pairs to present their designs, encouraging feedback on the eye-catching and persuasive qualities of the posters.

Differentiation
Support: Re-read the relevant text together and note on the board ideas for content before pairs design their posters.

Extension: Let pairs design another poster, such as one advertising Juglini's Circus, or a 'Wanted' poster for Jim, designed by Nick.

4. Dramatic scenes

Objective
To summarise the main ideas drawn from more than one paragraph.

What you need
Copies of *Street Child*, completed photocopiable page 37 'Jim's escape plan', photocopiable page 41 'Dramatic scenes'.

Cross-curricular link
Art and design

What to do

- Revisit the completed photocopiable page 37 'Jim's escape plan'.

- Tell the children to imagine that they are planning to film the escape scene for a movie. Explain that film-makers often make storyboards (a sequence of pictures showing how the action develops) before filming.

- Put the children into pairs and let them re-read Chapter 18, referring to the listed stages of Jim's escape plan on photocopiable page 37. Encourage them to decide on six scenes which they are going to illustrate for their storyboard.

- Hand out photocopiable page 41 'Dramatic scenes'. Tell the children to use the sheet to write notes for what each scene should depict. Encourage them to include detail such as sound effects (the distant pageant, Jim scraping the rope, the farmyard animals and so on) and close-up camera shots.

- Bring the class back together and write the best suggestions on the board. Encourage feedback. Ask: *Where could a close-up shot be effective?* (the rope finally snapping; Snipe's yellow eyes watching)

- Let the children, in their pairs, sketch the storyboard scenes they have briefed.

Differentiation
Support: Provide support in choosing the storyboard scenes and model on the board notes for one scene.

Extension: Let the children choose another episode from the novel and create a storyboard for it in notes and sketches.

5. Betsy's fine plan

Objective
To predict what might happen from details stated and implied.

What you need
Copies of *Street Child*, photocopiable page 42 'Betsy's fine plan'.

What to do

- Ask the children if they can recall when Jim first sees Barnie (when Lame Betsy takes Jim to hear him speak). Ask: *What is Jim's reaction?* (He is rude to Barnie and runs away as he hates the idea of school.)

- Tell them that they are going to work in small groups to script a play scene showing what happens when Betsy and Jim return home that day to Rosie. Ask: *What might Betsy tell Rosie and what might Jim say in his defence?*

- Arrange the children into groups of three. Hand out photocopiable page 42 'Betsy's fine plan' and explain to the children that they should use it as a planning sheet for their playscript. Allow them time to fill in the sheet, referring back to Chapter 12 to help them.

- When they have completed the sheet, they should first try to improvise a scene with each child playing a part. When they have rehearsed the scene, they should then draft it as a short playscript, starting with the lines shown at the bottom of photocopiable page 42.

Differentiation

Support: Read together the relevant part of Chapter 12 and discuss the questions on photocopiable page 42 before groups fill them in.

Extension: Let children perform their play scenes and freeze-frame them at different points, asking for constructive feedback.

6. Street sequel

Objective
To predict what might happen from details stated and implied.

What you need
Copies of *Street Child*, photocopiable page 43 'Street sequel'.

What to do

- Focus on the genre of the novel (adventure/historical novel). Can the children identify the key features of the genre? (a setting in the past, a central character facing difficulties alone and how he achieves his goal through stoicism and bravery and the help of others)

- Ask: *Can you identify the main theme of the story?* (the plight of street children in Victorian London; those who maltreated them and those who helped them)

- Tell them that the author wrote a sequel to the novel (*Far From Home*) about Jim's sisters. Ask: *What is a sequel?* Discuss examples of sequels using familiar books and films.

- Working in pairs, challenge the children to think of an idea for a sequel. Encourage them to explore different pathways (Jim might try to get Tip out of the workhouse; Grimy Nick might come looking for Jim). Ask the children, in their pairs, to make a list of the key ingredients that a sequel would need.

- Bring the class together to discuss their ideas. Write some headings on the board for different elements (for example, 'Facing dangers', 'Unexpected events', 'Conflict between characters').

- Let the children work on their own to complete photocopiable page 43 'Street sequel'.

Differentiation

Support: Develop one pathway for a sequel as a shared activity and let children continue to develop it using the photocopiable page.

Extension: Challenge children to write a few paragraphs of their sequel.

Dramatic scenes

- Use this storyboard to plan a film sequence showing how Jim escapes from Grimy Nick and Snipe. Make short notes on characters, setting and action before you plan each scene.

Character(s) _____

Setting _____

Action _____

1.	2.	3.
4.	5.	6.

Betsy's fine plan

- Use this sheet to help you plan a playscript about what happens when Lame Betsy and Jim return to Rosie after hearing Barnie speak.

- Discuss these questions and write some notes to answer them:

  1. What does Rosie feel about it?

  _____

  _____

  2. What does Jim feel about it?

  _____

  _____

  3. What does Jim do when he hears what the doctor says?

  _____

  _____

  4. Why do you think he reacts that way?

  _____

  _____

  5. How does the doctor respond and why?

  _____

  _____

- Use your plan to draft a play script. It can begin like this:

Lame Betsy:	Rosie, wait till you hear what Jim did!
Rosie:	Did you get to see the doctor, Jim?
Jim:	I saw him all right!

Street sequel

Write some notes for your sequel to *Street Child*.

Title of my sequel: _____

Who are the main characters?

_____

_____

_____

Where is the story set?

_____

_____

_____

Summarise what happens in the story.

_____

_____

_____

_____

_____

Explain how the story ends.

_____

_____

_____

_____

_____

ASSESSMENT ▶

1. What kind of novel?

> **Objective**
> To identify and discuss themes and conventions in a range of writing.
>
> **What you need**
> Copies of *Street Child*.

What to do

- Ask: *Which two genres does Street Child fit into?* (adventure and historical) Arrange the class into small groups. Assign each group one of the genres. Ask them to compile a list of the main features of their genre that the novel contains (for example, adventure – a journey or quest in search of something, overcoming villains and obstacles; historical – a real setting in past times). One member of each group should take notes.

- When they have finished, ask the groups to compile a second list of the main themes of their genre (for example, historical – poverty in Victorian England; adventure – an orphan facing troubles alone). When they have finished, ask all the groups for each genre to share their ideas. They should then work together to consolidate them into a list of up to five main features and five main themes.

- Bring the class back together and invite a volunteer for each genre to read aloud their lists, writing them on the board.

- Ask the children if they can suggest why Berlie Doherty and other authors (including Philip Pullman, Celia Rees and Rosemary Sutcliff) might use historical settings for adventure stories, and why readers would choose to read them.

> **Differentiation**
>
> **Support:** Let groups refer back to work from earlier lessons (Jim's journey).
>
> ---
>
> **Extension:** Ask groups to discuss another adventure story with an historical setting and list its main features and themes.

2. Read all about it

> **Objective**
> To identify the audience for and purpose of the writing, selecting the appropriate form and using other similar writing as models for their own.
>
> **What you need**
> Copies of *Street Child*.

What to do

- Ask a volunteer to read aloud the blurb from the back cover. Discuss the purpose of the blurb. Ask: *How does the blurb encourage us to read this novel?* (to find out what happens to Jim; to discover the dangers he faces and how he escapes them) *Does the blurb tell us anything else?* (where and when the novel is set, what kind of story it will be)

- Identify the key features of a blurb. (It needs to be concise, to summarise exciting or intriguing aspects of the novel and to raise questions in the readers' minds that we want answered: what dangers and troubles will Jim face? How will he overcome them? Will there be a happy ending?)

- Challenge pairs of children to draft their own blurb that would encourage readers to read the novel. Encourage them to try to identify different aspects of the novel (for example, Jim bravely facing dangers alone; his struggle for survival; the friendships he makes or the villains he encounters, such as Grimy Nick). Invite pairs to read their blurb to the class, encouraging constructive feedback.

> **Differentiation**
>
> **Support:** Guide children by giving them three specific areas to write about in their blurb.
>
> ---
>
> **Extension:** Ask pairs to design a book jacket, incorporating their blurb, to attract readers.

3. Keep it brief

Objective
To summarise the main ideas drawn from more than one paragraph.

What you need
Copies of *Street Child,* flash cards with names of key characters (Jim, Tip, Shrimps, Nick, Betsy, Rosie, Barnie), a stopwatch, photocopiable page 47 'Keep it brief'.

What to do
- Tell the children that they are going to try to summarise in as concise a way as possible how key characters are important to the plot. Explain that you will hold up flash cards with characters' names and volunteers should then summarise in as few words as possible, and in less than 30 seconds, how they are important to the plot. They should follow the same sentence pattern saying: 'Nick is important to the plot because…'

- Model one example for them: 'Nick is important to the plot because he buys Jim from Rosie's grandfather and makes him work on the coal lighter.'

- Challenge each volunteer to summarise the key points of their character in less than 30 seconds, using the stopwatch to limit the time.

- Tell the children that they are now going to do the same exercise focusing on objects that feature in the plot. Hand out photocopiable page 47 'Keep it brief' and explain to the children that they should write notes explaining why each object is important to the plot. They should then cut out and place the pictures in the order they appear in the plot. In pairs, allow children time to complete the activity.

Differentiation
Support: Before children begin the written work, ask them to discuss in pairs the context of each item on the photocopiable page.

Extension: Challenge children to extend the activity by sketching other items that feature in the plot and then briefly explaining their significance.

4. Emotional rollercoaster

Objective
To explain and discuss their understanding of what they have read.

What you need
Copies of *Street Child.*

Cross-curricular link
PSHE

What to do
- Invite volunteers to recall different emotions that Jim feels during the course of the novel (sadness, fear, excitement and so on). List their suggestions on the board.

- Choose one emotion and begin writing a sentence on the board (for example, 'sad': 'Jim feels sad when _____.') Invite a volunteer to complete the sentence (for example, 'Jim feels sad when his mother dies.') Encourage volunteers to suggest other times when Jim feels sad (for example, 'Jim feels sad when Shrimps dies.')

- Arrange the children into pairs. Challenge them to draft sentences following the same pattern and using as many of the adjectives listed on the board as possible. Explore a variety of emotions including fear, happiness and excitement using the sentence starter 'Jim feels _____' each time.

- Explain that for this task they should work from their knowledge and memory of the plot.

- Bring the class back together and invite pairs to read out their sentences. Ask: *How much variety is there in your answers? Which emotions seem to dominate?* (fear, sadness) *How does Jim feel at the beginning of the story? And at the end?* (excited, contented)

Differentiation
Support: Allow pairs of children to refer back to the novel to help them find examples.

Extension: Encourage children to use a thesaurus to explore a range of vocabulary for their sentences (such as 'afraid', 'scared', 'fearful', 'anxious', 'worried', 'content').

ASSESSMENT

5. Street-wise quiz

Objective
To ask questions to improve their understanding.

What you need
Copies of *Street Child*.

What to do

- Tell the children that they are going to compile a true-or-false quiz about the novel to challenge other groups or teams. Arrange them into small groups and give them time to compile a quiz of six true-or-false statements. Children should skim and scan the novel for ideas. They should appoint one note-taker to write down their ideas and another to keep a list of correct answers.

- Before they begin, model examples on the board: 'Lame Betsy is a cook.' (Answer – false); 'Shrimps sells bootlaces to earn money.' (Answer – true).

- Once groups have thought of six statements, they can then challenge each other to answer their quiz. Again, they will need to appoint a note-taker to count correct or incorrect answers. When they have finished, review scores and announce winning teams or groups.

- Encourage feedback, identifying which quiz questions were most challenging and why (for example, recalling exact detail about characters or the correct sequence of events).

- If there is time, allow groups to compete in a Spelling Bee challenge. Each should compile six of the most tricky spellings that they can find in the novel and challenge other groups to spell them from memory.

Differentiation

Support: Let children concentrate on one topic such as characters in the novel or one setting such as the workhouse.

Extension: Ask groups of children to devise a more challenging quiz about the novel, for example, a quiz consisting of multiple-choice questions.

6. Victorian glossary

Objective
To understand that the spelling of some words needs to be learned specifically.

What you need
Copies of *Street Child*, dictionaries.

Cross-curricular link
History

What to do

- Tell the children that they are going to compile a glossary of words and terms which will help readers understand the author's references to the period of the novel (the 1860s). Ask: *Does anyone know the dates of Queen Victoria's reign?* (1837–1901)

- Arrange the children into small groups. Assign each group four or five chapters and tell them to skim and scan each chapter for any words which relate to something specifically Victorian, which readers today might not instantly recognise or understand (for example, a shilling, the workhouse, a slate, a pageant, a coal lighter, ragged school).

- Groups should skim and scan the chapters together and appoint a note-taker to list all of the words they can find. They should then draft together a definition for that word which would explain it clearly and concisely to readers who are unfamiliar with the word or the era.

- When the groups have finished, let them use their word lists to test other groups on tricky spellings and meanings.

- Bring the class together to allow groups to share their findings and to compile a class Victorian glossary to the novel.

- Review the glossary as a class, encouraging children to edit and improve their work.

Differentiation

Support: Allow children to use dictionaries to help them compile their glossaries.

Extension: Challenge groups to use their own reading and research to extend their Victorian glossaries.

Keep it brief

Working with a partner, talk about how each object features in *Street Child*.

Cut out and place the pictures in the order they appear in the novel.

Available in this series:

978-1407-15879-2

978-1407-14224-1

978-1407-16063-4

978-1407-16056-6

978-1407-14228-9

978-1407-16069-6

978-1407-16070-2

978-1407-16071-9

978-1407-14230-2

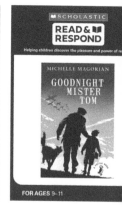

978-1407-16057-3

978-1407-16064-1

978-1407-14223-4

978-0702-30890-1

978-0702-30859-8

To find out more,
visit www.scholastic.co.uk/read-and-respond